THE COVERING

BERT CINTRON

Divine Works Publishing, LLC

© 2025 Bert Cintron

All Rights Reserved. No part of this publication may be reproduced, stored in a retrieval system, or transmitted in any form or by any means, electronic, mechanical, photocopying, recording or otherwise without the prior permission of the publisher or in accordance with the provisions of the Copyright, Designs, and Patents Act 1988 or under the terms of any license permitting limited copying issued by the Copyright Licensing Agency.

The views expressed in this work are solely those of the author and do not necessarily reflect the views of the publisher. The publisher hereby disclaims any responsibility for them.

ISBN: 978-1-949105-87-2 (paperback)
ISBN: 978-1-949105-88-9 (eBook)

Library of Congress Control Number:
2025913310

First Edition Published: 07/02/2025
Printed: Royal Palm Beach, Florida, United States

Sources Cited: Scriptures by King James Version (KJV) unless otherwise noted. **Holy Bible, New Living Translation,** copyright © 1996, 2004, 2015 by Tyndale House Foundation. Used by permission of Tyndale House Publishers, Inc., Carol Stream, Illinois 60188. All Rights Reserved. **Holy Bible, New International Version®, NIV®** Copyright ©1973, 1978, 1984, 2011 by Biblica, Inc.® Used by permission. All Rights Reserved.

Divine Works Publishing books are available at special discounts when purchased in quantity for premiums and promotions and for educational and fundraising use. For details, feel free contact us via email:
books@divineworkspublishing.com or call the number listed below.

Published by:
Divine Works Publishing
Royal Palm Beach, Florida USA
www.DivineWorksPublishing.com
561-990-BOOK (2665)

Dedication

I dedicate this book to both of my grandmas—Petra Medina Ortiz, who prophesied over my destiny, and Tomasa Medina, who covered me in prayer, inspired by the Spirit of God. Together, they became an unbreakable blanket of spiritual protection that enveloped me all the days of my life. That covering sealed me until everything God poured into me could be poured out to others—not by my might, nor by my strength, but by the Spirit of the living God.

This book is for everyone who has been covered by their grandmother's prayers and for the grandmother's and mother's still waiting for the miracles they pray over their loved ones to be made manifest. May this book re-ignite your faith and prayer life with renewed passion.

The Covering - A Spoken Word

I wasn't just born into pain—I was born with a purpose.
Every scar. Every tear. Every fight I thought I lost.
It wasn't punishment.
It wasn't fate.
It was preparation.

I was called to walk through darkness,
not to be consumed by it—but to survive it,
to carry light back into it, and to lead others out.

You see, God didn't just rescue me.
He raised me in the fire.

He lit a flame in me
the streets couldn't steal,
prison couldn't chain,
addiction couldn't drown,
and pain couldn't put out.

This isn't the story of a man who made it on his own.
This is the story of a God who protects, provides, and promotes;
even from the darkest places.

I was born in the pain,
called by the flame,
and sent in His Name.

This book is for the ones still fighting in the fire.

Hold on.
The Light is coming for you too.

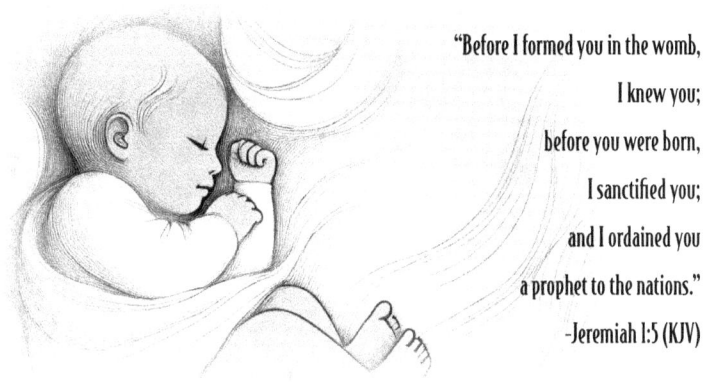

"Before I formed you in the womb,
I knew you;
before you were born,
I sanctified you;
and I ordained you
a prophet to the nations."
-Jeremiah 1:5 (KJV)

Early Life and Family Struggles

The author describes his chaotic upbringing, one filled with abuse, domestic violence and shame. He recounts the fear experienced during his father's violent outbursts and the helplessness felt by his siblings.

A pivotal moment occurred when he witnessed his mother being violently attacked, leading him to reflect on his own lack of compassion in that moment. This reflection revealed a deep-seated anger towards women, stemming from past abuse, which God later helped him better understand.

Shame Sets In

One day, when I was six years old, my mother said, "Hijo (Spanish for *son*), today we are going to church." I begged my mother, saying, "I can't go. I don't even have clean clothes to wear." No matter how much I begged her not to bring me, we went anyway (if you have a Puerto Rican mother and you're six years old, you know I didn't stand a chance).

So while I was there, I suddenly began running around the church. The people there and my mother tried to stop me from running around. I just kept running. The pastor warned them, "Leave him alone. It is the Holy Spirit causing this, not him." The room went still. Nobody tried to stop me after that.

The Understanding: Later, as I was recovering, I asked God to explain what happened that day in the church, and He began to reveal it to me. He said, "That was the day I anointed you to go through all you would go through in order to fulfill what I've called you to do."

The scripture He gave me to back this up was the story of when the prophet Samuel anointed David—not just for kingship, but for the battles he would face against lions, bears, and eventually Goliath.

You see, God anoints you even for the bad things you must go through so that you can eventually come out of the path of darkness and into God's marvelous light, and eventually help those who have not yet faced their own lions, bears, and Goliaths.

The Shame Starts

My next experience was at Sunday School. I was doing what I always did—trying to make people laugh. The teacher grabbed me by my feet, turned me upside down, and began to swing me around. All the children began to laugh but this time, the laughter wasn't with me; it was at me.

The Understanding: Later, God revealed to me that this was where shame first began to take its grip on me.

Spiritual Root: Shame

Key Verse: *"So now there is no condemnation for those who belong to Christ Jesus."* –Romans 8:1 (NLT)

Branches: Hiding or masking true self, Self-hatred, Perfectionism, Fear of exposure, Inability to receive love, Toxic comparison, Victim mentality

Reflections for the reader:

- What moments or memories make me feel most ashamed?
- In what ways have I hidden my true self to avoid being seen, rejected, or judged?
- What lies of self-hatred have I believed, and how have they shaped how I treat myself or expect others to treat me?
- What does it mean for me to walk in freedom from shame?

"For you created my inmost being;
You knit me together in my mother's womb.
I praise you because I am fearfully
and wonderfully made;"
-Psalm 139:14 (NIV)

2

Family Hurts

The author recalls traumatic memories of domestic violence in his childhood home. He describes nights when fights between his parents would occur, leading to fear and distress among the children, particularly the sister who would shake and urinate from fear. One incident is highlighted where the father severely injured their mother, prompting him to selfishly consider taking her belongings—reflecting on a lack of love and support for her during such critical moments.

When Hurt People Hurt People

I remember late nights when my dad came home, and we knew there was going to be a fight between him and my mom. We would huddle together and squeeze each other tight. My sister would become so scared that she would start to shake and urinate on herself.

I recall one of those nights when my younger brother had seen enough of my mom getting beaten. He tried to stop my dad by jumping on his back, but that didn't stop anything. It bred more hopelessness instead.

I remember another night, during another fight, when my dad came into the house and hit my mom so hard it knocked her out. My first reaction wasn't to help my mom, but to go into her dresser to see what I could take of hers for myself. In my mind, she would no longer need it. Looking back, I questioned myself: where was the love for my mother when she needed it the most?

The Understanding: In recovery, God began to reveal to me a picture: it was of a kid who looked to be around seven years old, lying on a bed, with a woman standing over him, beginning to take his clothes off. That's where God stopped showing me the picture and now I know it was for my protection; to avoid any further injuries—I wasn't ready to face it. Then God said, "That kid was you."

He didn't show me the abuse itself—just enough for me to know that I was abused. While the other family members were outside the room, there was one inside. You see, most abuse starts at home or from a family member.

This is when God revealed to me how I could walk away from my mother and have no love to give her when she needed it the most.

God explained, "By this time, you had so much anger in your heart toward women because of the bad experiences you endured by the one woman who hurt you. By then, the damage was done to your heart. That's why there was no compassion left to give."

Spiritual Root: Bitterness

Key Verse: *"Get rid of all bitterness, rage and anger... Be kind and compassionate to one another, forgiving each other, just as in Christ God forgave you."*
– *Ephesians 4:31-32*

Branches: Unforgiveness, Resentment and grudges, Anger and passive-aggressiveness, Sarcasm and cynicism, Envy or comparison Internal torment (emotional pain, sleeplessness) Victim mindset

Reflections for the reader:

- Is there someone I still feel anger, resentment, or pain toward?
- What unresolved wounds might be feeding bitterness in my heart?
- How has bitterness affected my ability to trust or love God and to trust or love others?

> "For God knew His people in advance, and He chose them to become like his Son, so that His Son would be the firstborn among many brothers and sisters. And having chosen them, He called them to come to Him. And having called them, he gave them right standing with himself. And having given them right standing, he gave them his glory."
> —Romans 8:29-30 (NLT)

3

The Cost of Freedom

At thirteen, the author felt a sense of freedom when his father left, which led him to associate with gang members and experiment with drugs. His introduction to cocaine resulted in an overdose, which he narrowly survived. This incident marked the beginning of a destructive cycle of addiction and anger, rooted in feelings of rejection and abandonment from his father's absence.

What Was the True Cost?

When my dad finally left, I was about thirteen. It was sad to see him go but at the same time, a surge of freedom rushed over me, like I could finally do whatever I wanted. It didn't take long. Right after that, I started hanging around with the gang members on the corner and eventually, I became one of them.

One night, I followed them to a run-down apartment. They pulled out an ounce of cocaine, tossing it onto the table like it was nothing. I watched for a second, then grabbed a line and snorted it, just like they did. Line after line. Hit after hit. Until everything went black.

The next thing I remember, I was being lifted off the ground. I could hear their muffled voices, but I couldn't make out what they were saying. My body was limp. I didn't know it then, but I had overdosed.

Where I come from, you don't call for help — you get rid of the evidence. They were carrying me toward the dumpster.

Suddenly, I opened my eyes. They began jamming their fingers in my throat to prevent me from swallowing my tongue. I thought they were trying to kill me because I had no knowledge of what overdosing was (at that time), so I looked around and asked in my weak voice "What are you doing? Where are you taking me?"

One of them answered, flat and cold, "We thought you were dead. We were just getting rid of the evidence."

I didn't argue. I didn't ask questions.

I understood "the code."

The Understanding: Now, looking back, I see what I couldn't see then — that the day my dad walked out, something cracked inside me.

The anger. The bitterness. They started growing roots the moment he closed the door behind him. I didn't recognize it at thirteen, but as a man, I can see how deep those roots went—how it poisoned everything. The rejection. The abandonment. It paralyzed me from the inside and gave birth to unforgiveness. The unforgiveness then chained me without me even knowing it.

Spiritual Root: Unforgiveness

Key Verse: *"For if you forgive other people when they sin against you, your heavenly Father will also forgive you. But if you do not forgive others their sins, your Father will not forgive your sins." –Matthew 6:14-15*

Branches: Retaliation or revenge fantasies, Emotional numbness or coldness, Isolation, Inability to trust others, Chronic stress or emotional heaviness, Replaying offenses mentally, Anger and rage, delayed healing (physically and/or emotionally).

Reflections for the reader:

- Who am I struggling to forgive right now? Why?
- What emotions rise up when I think of that person or situation?
- Have I believed any lies that keep me holding onto this offense?
- What might it cost me to keep holding onto unforgiveness?
- What would it look like for me to truly release this to God?

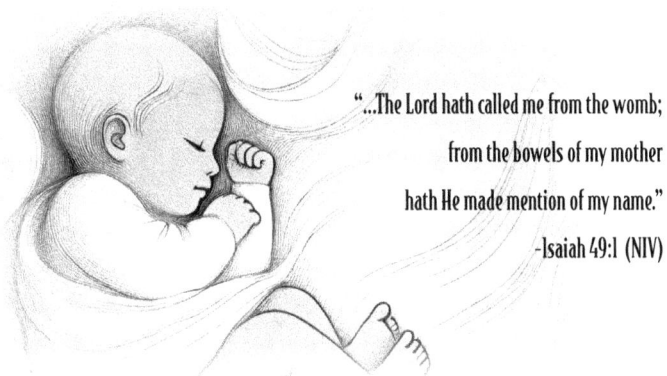

"...The Lord hath called me from the womb; from the bowels of my mother hath He made mention of my name."
-Isaiah 49:1 (NIV)

4

Divine Interventions

Throughout his struggles, the author experienced several moments of divine intervention. He recounts one specific life-threatening instance where he was being chased by gang members but was miraculously protected by two pit bulls, symbolizing unyielding God's grace and mercy. Additionally, he reflects on a time when he was saved from a potential beating by a stranger who recognized him, further illustrating God's protective hand in his life.

Divine Rescues - Realities of Street Life

One morning, I woke up sick as a dog, shaking, sweating, withdrawing. I weighed maybe 90 pounds. All I knew was that I needed a fix, and at that point, it didn't matter what I had to do to get it. I stumbled to a corner I knew, early in the morning when the streets were still waking up.

I waited, hoping one of the regulars would show up so I could sell them a beat bag—fake dope—just long enough to get real dope for myself. But I got spotted.

The dealers who ran that corner—eight black guys—saw me hustling on their turf. They came after me. Fear gripped me like a vice, but somehow, even in my frail, withdrawing body, there was just enough strength to run.

I bolted.

With every step, it felt like the little life I had left inside me was leaking out. My legs were giving up. My chest was on fire.

I turned the corner and there it was: a ten-foot fence standing between me and escape.

I closed my eyes.

And when I opened them, somehow, someway, I was already on the other side. I looked back. The guys who had been chasing me stood frozen, their eyes wide, their mouths open like they had seen a ghost.

I didn't understand why. Not until I looked down.

Standing on each side of me, close enough to touch, were two pit bulls—one on my right, one on my left.

My heart stopped.

Let me be clear: pit bulls in the hood aren't house pets—they're trained to kill. But these two didn't growl, didn't bark, didn't even move toward me.

They just stood there.

And the guys who had been ready to beat me down — they backed off and disappeared without ever laying a hand on me.

The Understanding: After a time in recovery God began to open my eyes to see his hand in this situation and began to reveal to me that His angels who he had given charge over me to keep me safe in all my ways had lifted me over that fence because there was definitely no way in my conditions that I have could have been able to get over that fence. God said that one of the pit bulls was Grace and the other pit bull Mercy. This was a picture of the angels that he had assigned to watch over me and keep me safe in all my ways all the days of my life.

I Need a Fix

There came another time when I needed a fix. So, I did the only thing I knew how to do—I went out to rob somebody.

I went to another corner to look for a victim, when all of a sudden, I became the victim.

A car pulled up, and about six guys jumped out and surrounded me. They started accusing me of ripping a chain off one of their girlfriends' necks.

Now, I had done that kind of thing before — but this time, I really hadn't.

As far as they were concerned, though, I was guilty.

The next words I heard were, "We're going to kill you."

Right after that, another voice broke through:

"Leave him alone. I know him."

Just like that, they all backed off—even the one who spoke up.

I honestly didn't know who he was. I caught a quick glance of his face but didn't see it clearly.

Years later, I was scrolling through Facebook and saw his face.

I remembered he was the one who had been there that day and had yelled, "Leave him alone."

His name was Moses. In the Bible, Moses was the deliverer of God's people.

As God continued to restore my relationship with Him, He brought that memory back to me.

He revealed that His hand had always been over my life that even when I didn't know it, He was there.

Always protecting me. Always sending a "Moses" one way or another to rescue me.

Spiritual Root: Addiction (Root or Fruit of Pain/Trauma)
Key Verses:
1 Corinthians 6:12 – "...I will not be mastered by anything."
Romans 6:16 – "You are slaves to the one you obey..."
John 8:36 – "So if the Son sets you free, you will be free indeed."

Branches: Substance abuse, Sexual addiction, Food addiction (gluttony or restriction), Codependency, Gambling, shopping, screen addiction, Escapism, Compulsive behaviors, Idolizing comfort

Reflections for the reader:
- What do I run to for comfort instead of God?
- How has this behavior affected my spiritual life?
- What steps can I take to invite Jesus into this struggle?

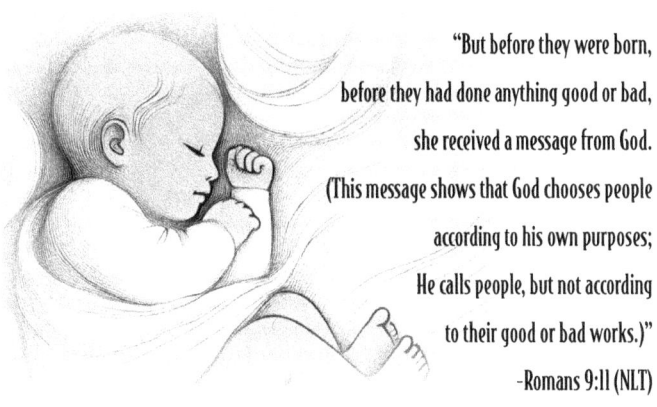

> "But before they were born, before they had done anything good or bad, she received a message from God. (This message shows that God chooses people according to his own purposes; He calls people, but not according to their good or bad works.)"
> -Romans 9:11 (NLT)

5

Beyond Just Jailhouse Conversion

After multiple run-ins with the law, the author was sentenced to prison, where he began to seek God. He describes a transformative experience during a prison riot when he prayed for protection and miraculously received it. Undeniably, the hand of God once again. This period of incarceration in turn became a time of spiritual awakening and preparation for his future.

Physically Imprisoned & Spiritually Bound

You would have thought that going through all this I would have gotten it or had learned my lessons **but when the mind is getting its information from a broken heart rather than a healed heart the results always come back broken**, as a man thinks in his heart, so is he. Because of my broken thinking still being in charge and still running my life, the word of God continued to intervene in my life—like the scripture that reads "my people are destroyed for lack of knowledge. I lacked knowledge of the truth, so the lies I held on to had every right to hold me as a prisoner.

With that being said, I recall a time that I bought a gun and started shooting it in the air while sitting on my mom's porch. About an hour later a police car drives by real slow and all of a sudden they jumped out I got up and ran in the house and threw the gun down the basement by then the cops had me down on the ground where it became a wrestling match and there is where I got charged with assaulting a police officer but at the end as we know I was the one that ended up with the handcuffs. So, with that charge and other charges pending I was sentenced to do about 3 years in prison but while in the county jail I became a member of the Latin Kings gang. So now I do about six months and then get transferred to prison. While I was there, I started seeking God. Like we do when we find ourselves in trouble. Some people would call it a "jailhouse conversion." But God even met me there.

After a period of time, a war broke out in the prison. And once again I went to God. I asked Him if he did not want me to get involved and do the right thing, then to make a way out for me. Because If I'm told to shank someone then I must do it. If not what I don't do would have been done to me, so I left it at that.

The next day I walked into the mess hall, and I looked around and no one was there but one person and believe it or not it was the leader of the Latin Kings. I walked towards him and He turned around and said "Bert, sit with me." He looked me straight in my eyes after I sat down and said "I want you to go home, so no matter what breaks out don't get involved."

The Understanding: Once again as you can now see through my life experiences, God truly makes a way when or where there seems to be no way. Now, I know that every time I was incarcerated that it wasn't by my hands neither by the hands of man but by the hands of God Himself, to preserve my life for such a time as this. Just as he did with Joseph, in order to help feed his people physically in the same way we feed God's people through spiritual <u>truth</u> (that sets the captives free—like me). When we agree with a lie, even silently, we give the enemy legal ground to build strongholds in our thinking.

Spiritual Root: Strongholds of the mind

Key Verse: *"We use God's mighty weapons, not worldly weapons, to knock down the strongholds of human reasoning and to destroy false arguments."*
—*2 Cor 10:4 (NLT)*

"And you will know the truth, and the truth will set you free."
—*John 8:32 (NLT)*

Branches: *Belief systems* built around deception that feel true because they've been reinforced emotionally, mentally, or socially.

Fear-based strongholds — where fear drives a person to trust in lies that feel "safer" than truth. Fear often partners with lies to create internal bondage: fear of being unloved, abandoned, failing, or being punished.

Reflections for the reader:

Deliverance from strongholds (lies within) begins with:

- Identifying the lie (e.g., "I'm not good enough")
- Renouncing the lie in Jesus' name
- Replacing it with God's truth (e.g., "I am fearfully and wonderfully made" —Psalm 139:14)
- Inviting the Holy Spirit to heal the wound where the lie entered
- Walking in community and accountability to stay grounded to trust or love others?

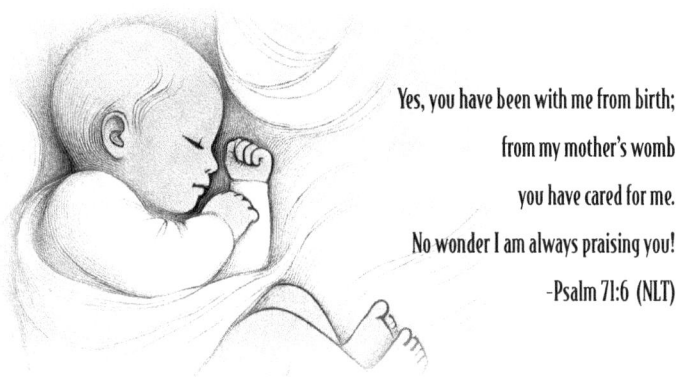

> Yes, you have been with me from birth;
> from my mother's womb
> you have cared for me.
> No wonder I am always praising you!
> –Psalm 71:6 (NLT)

6

Life After Prison

Upon release from prison, the author initially struggled with sobriety but he eventually sought help through a detox program. A significant moment occurred during a prayer session when he realized he had not fully accepted God into his heart due to unresolved brokenness. This realization led to a deeper understanding of his need for healing and a true relationship with God, culminating in a profound sense of freedom.

Released—but Not Free

Newly out of prison, I didn't pick up any drugs for about six months. I began working the night shift at a fence-painting factory. One night, I started getting high. On this day before work, I did a few bags and drank some alcohol, so by the time I got to work, I was already feeling very high. While at work—to add to it—I began sniffing paint thinner, and before I knew it, I was outside the factory, just walking around upset and crying because once again, I had ruined another job and realized I had done exactly what I swore I would never do again.

I picked up alcohol and drugs.

I said to myself, "I can't do this anymore." As I walked, I saw a church on the corner having a service, and I had heard that's where people go to get help and I definitely felt like I needed help! I was tired and really believed that I was done, but later, that belief would reveal itself as a lie—a lie I truly believed at the time was true.

When I got there, I saw a guy praying for people in a line, so I jumped in line to get prayer. When he finally stood in front of me, the only thing that came out of his mouth was, "You aren't finished yet."

So I left disappointed like we all do, one way or another, when things don't go our way.

The Understanding: What I understand now that I didn't understand before is that God spoke through man. This guy didn't even know me. That night, God Himself, through that man, spoke to me and told me I wasn't done yet walking through the path of darkness. The proof of that was that I continued down the path of darkness for two more years, until He called me out into His marvelous light.

You see, before the foundations of the earth, even before I was conceived in my mother's womb, He knew me and planned to send me into the world to go through whatever I needed to go through, so that He could bring me out and begin restoration. One day, I would be used as His vessel—an instrument He could work through to help restore others from death to life.

So, think about whether your life is an accident or on purpose.

He who has begun a good work in you is faithful to complete it. The proof of that is my life. He continues to work out my life so that He can completely live His through mine—it is no longer my life, but His.

In the process of recovering, God continued doing things here and there, just to reveal who He is to me in different forms.

Spiritual Root: Trauma & Unhealed Pain

Key Verse: *"He heals the brokenhearted and binds up their wounds." – Psalm 147:3* (Addiction is used to escape unresolved emotional wounds or abuse, whether remembered or repressed.)

Branches: Substance abuse, fantasy/escapism, sleep or screen addiction, disassociation. (emotional pain, sleeplessness) Victim mindset

Reflections for the reader:

- What am I really trying to escape, numb, or feel in control of when I turn to this addiction?
- What lie or wound could be driving the need to keep returning to something I know doesn't satisfy?

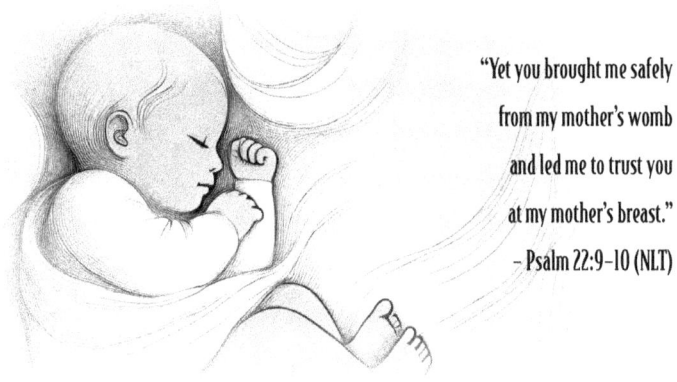

"Yet you brought me safely
from my mother's womb
and led me to trust you
at my mother's breast."
– Psalm 22:9-10 (NLT)

7

Recovered and Reset

On his journey of recovery from alcohol addiction, the author emphasizes the importance of forgiveness and self-worth, reflecting on how unforgiveness served as a major barrier to healing by hindering progress and blocking the freedom that comes from God.

A significant dream revealed deep-seated feelings of unworthiness rooted in unmet emotional needs from the author's relationship with his father, illustrating how such unresolved wounds can prevent one from fully accepting the good things in life and embracing true transformation.

An Earnest Desire to Heal

So, later, after two years of recovering from alcohol addiction, I wanted to give up. As I was crying and arguing with God, telling Him that I felt that AA or Church was not working for me, He opened my eyes to see that the reason why I felt like I couldn't move forward was because He never moved me forward. He couldn't because unforgiveness was blocking me from being able to move forward. In my head, I believed the lie that I forgave the person I had a bad experience with, but it was a head thing, never a heart thing. "You see, the person you had a bad experience with didn't have the security, the love, or the care that you really longed for. And because they themselves were broken and never received it from their parents they were not able to give it. So, because of that revelation, I understood what God was telling me. With that, like that person who I had a bad experience with never got a chance to experience with God himself: Freedom. The Lord will now begin to deal with the root cause of the real problem in your life.

The Understanding: I remember feeling unworthy even when good things began to happen in my life. The more I received, the more unworthy I felt. Then I went to God about it. After a few weeks, I had a dream. In the dream, my dad was in the center of a circle, and the circle was made up of kids all around it. Then I saw my dad begin to give out money and candy to all the kids one by one. I was one of the kids in that circle, and by the time he got to me, he had nothing to give me. God began to reveal to me what I longed for from my dad—the love, the security, the safety that I longed for, as we all do—he didn't have to give me because he himself was broken. So, in the dream, I believed the lie that if my dad didn't think I deserved anything, then I didn't. There was the root cause for me feeling unworthy to receive anything good. I share this to help someone who doesn't know what it is for God to deal with the root cause in your own life. The truth is that we repeat what we don't allow God to heal or process us through in our very own life. But He came to free you and me from our life in order to experience true life.

Spiritual Root: Unworthiness

The root of unworthiness is a deeply embedded lie that often begins in childhood or trauma and causes people to live beneath their God-given identity. It can block intimacy with God, distort relationships, and fuel cycles of addiction, performance, people-pleasing, or self-sabotage.

Key Verses: *"But God demonstrates His own love for us in this: While we were still sinners, Christ died for us." –Romans 5:8*

"He saved us, not because of righteous things we had done, but because of His mercy…" –Titus 3:5

"Do not fear, for I have redeemed you; I have called you by name; you are mine." –Isaiah 43:1

Branches: Self-hatred/self-rejection, People-pleasing/approval addiction, Inability to receive love or blessings, Performance-based identity, Self-sabotage, Depression or apathy, Victim mindset, Over-apologizing, Shrinking back from purpose or calling, Comparison to others, Feeling like a burden, Guilt without grace

Reflections for the reader:

- What messages or experiences first made me feel I wasn't good enough, worthy of love, or valuable? (Reflect on childhood relationships, criticism, abandonment, or trauma.)
- What would change in my life if I fully believed I was already loved, chosen, and accepted by God? (Let the Holy Spirit show you what your healed identity looks like.)

"Did not he that made me in the womb make him? and did not one fashion us in the womb?"
—Job 31:15 (NLT)

8

New Jersey – New Life

The author reflects on his ongoing journey of personal recovery and a deep desire to help friends in New Jersey.

Initially eager to assist others, he soon realized he was not ready to help until he had fully experienced his own healing.

This experience teaches him that the timing of helping others is determined only by God, highlighting that one should not rush to save everyone, but instead wait for the right opportunities as guided by divine insight and divine timing.

Jersey Bound and Rebound

After some time in the process of recovering, I suddenly had a desire to go to Jersey and help my friends. I wanted them to experience what I was experiencing. But I didn't realize at the time that I wasn't really ready to help anyone change, because I was still in the process of being changed myself and didn't have much to offer yet. I was still just beginning to believe in the One who was still changing me, because if I wasn't healed first, I would have only gotten in the way of helping anyone else properly.

So anyway, I went, planning to stay there for a month helping others, but after about two weeks of trying, I just wanted to give up on people altogether, go back home, and never try to help anyone again.

You see, the desire I had was a God-given desire, because there was a lesson in it for me. Without going through that experience, I would have never learned that one broken person can't properly help another broken person—and that I'm not called to save everyone. Only those He has assigned for me to help, at His timing, not mine.

The Understanding: What He taught me through this was that just because others look like they need help doesn't mean they are ready for help and that truth freed me from feeling like I had to save the world.

Spiritual Root: Pride or Self-Reliance

(When we feel we must make it happen ourselves apart from God's process —we may be driven by ego or a desire for control.)

Key Verses: *"God resists the proud, but gives grace unto the humble."*
—*James 4:6*

Branches: Distrust in God's provision or pace; anxiety about being left behind.

Reflections for the reader:

- In what ways do I rely more on my own efforts than on divine guidance? (Do I treat prayer as a last resort or a first response?)
- What might God want to show me in the space where I release control to Him? (How can I trust in God's perfect plan for me?)
- Do I secretly equate asking God for help with failure? Why? (What belief do I need to unlearn about doing things all on my own?)

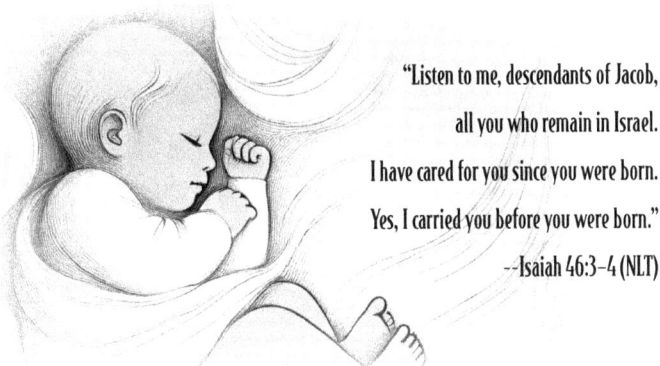

"Listen to me, descendants of Jacob,
all you who remain in Israel.
I have cared for you since you were born.
Yes, I carried you before you were born."
--Isaiah 46:3-4 (NLT)

9

God Provides and Proves Himself

The author recognizes God's constant presence and provision throughout his life, even during the most difficult of times. Accentuating the importance of changing one's mindset to align with the understanding that God meets needs according to one's level of thinking—highlighting a transformative relationship with faith.

God Always Provides

In the process of God restoring my relationship back to Himself, He began to show me that He was always with me, that even when I slept in abandoned houses or had a meal from the hands of others, it had been Him providing for me.

Here he was showing me not only that He was always with me but also that He was always meeting my needs and how He met my needs according to the level of my thinking.

The Bible says *"as a man thinks a man is."* In other words, he met me at the level of my thinking and that's why my thinking had to change. You see, even before I knew God as the provider of my needs, He was already providing for my needs.

God Shows Me How Much He Loves Me

God started showing me—for instance, I was working with another brother in Christ, and daily we would help build each other up. One day, he started talking about Cadillacs and said he feels that God is going to give him a white Cadillac one day. In my head, I was like, "Whatever," but deep inside, I knew what he was speaking was coming from God.

One day, his car started acting up, and he said, "I don't know how much longer I'll be able to drive this car." I told him, "Don't worry, because when this one breaks down, God is going to give you that Cadillac."

After about three months, he called me and told me to come help him push his car off the road because it had broken down. I started laughing, and he got mad. He said, "Brother, did you just hear what I said?" I replied, "Yeah, I'm laughing from excitement because now God is going to give you the Cadillac."

So we left the job one day, and I'm on my way home. I hear God speak to me, and He said, "Call Bryan and tell him to meet you at Starbucks tomorrow afternoon." We met the next day and were sitting down drinking coffee. All of a sudden, I felt the atmosphere change, and I looked up and saw a man sitting across from us. God said, "Don't judge him," and I guess that was because he had a cigarette in his mouth.

That same guy got up, walked toward us, and said, "I have a car that God wants me to give you." We looked at each other with unbelief—you know, when things really happen that you didn't really believe deep inside could happen, and then they do happen.

So the guy says the car was out front. We walked out, and guess what kind of car it was? A white Cadillac. He not only gave him the car but filled up his gas tank and gave him $200 to change the title over to his name.

Then the man's wife showed up to the scene and sat at the table with us. She handed me a check, and when I saw the amount, it was exactly the price of the phone. After I saw the amount, I heard God say, "Now go get your phone."

The reason why God said that was because the day before this happened, the new iPhone had just come out. I picked one up and looked at it. God said, "Get it," and I didn't because I let the fear that was working with insecurity in my life at the time stop me. I had no clue because it was hidden in a dark place that I could not see at the time—until the proper time when God would open my eyes to see the defects in my character for what they really were (without me using it against myself), because I didn't have the wisdom to know the difference between who I was and who I wasn't.

You see, God was developing real faith in me, the kind of faith that would eventually override the doubt in me. The doubt that worked through brokenness and broken feelings rather than healing the insecurity that kept me living with doubt. God has a way of teaching us to walk by faith and not by sight.

Unexpected Tax Bill

So, there came a day when I got a letter saying that I had to pay $600 in taxes. I had never paid taxes in my life, and I really didn't want to do it now, but I wanted to do the next right thing, so I prayed about it. I told God, "I don't have the $600, and if you want me to pay it, you'll have to make a way." The next day, I got a call from somebody that needed work done in their yard. So, I went there, and he wanted me to cut a few branches here and there. When I was done, this guy gave me a check. I looked at it and it was exactly $600 what I needed to pay my taxes and I had never mentioned anything about or the amount I needed. It sounds like a lot for such little work, but this little became bigger in God's hands. So, this guy said, "I have more work for you if you want it." I wanted to yell, "If I want it? I'll be here at three in the morning!" So, anyways, I did.

More Blessings and Miracles

I continued to do more work for him, and one day as I was working he called me over to have a soda with him. I told him, "You have no idea what a blessing you are to me." I didn't know if he believed in God or not, but I told him that I asked God to bless him in whatever it is that he needed it the most. So, after that, I left, and I came back about two days later. He called me over and said, "I didn't know if you knew this, but I had cancer, and the doctors called me and told me that now they couldn't find a trace of it." Whether he knew it or not, I knew God gave him what no man could—it was divine healing.

Another time when I came back, he called me over again and told me that he had another house and that some of the electricity burned out, and it was going to cost him $2000.31 to get it fixed. He said a miracle happened. He didn't see the miracle with the cancer, but he saw it when it hit his pocket. God knows us better than we know ourselves. Then he said, "I got a check in the mail for a back payment from social security, and guess how much it was? It was $2000.31."

Understanding: Once again, the hand of God through little miracles here and there were used by God to help my unbelief.

Spiritual Root: Unbelief

Unbelief often partners with fear, rejection, and pride, and is at times passed generationally via religious or skeptical mindsets.

Key Verses: *"Beware... lest there be in any of you an evil heart of unbelief in departing from the living God."* –Hebrews 3:12

"Lord, I believe; help my unbelief!" –Mark 9:24

"And without faith it is impossible to please God..." –Hebrews 11:6

"The one who doubts is like a wave of the sea... That person should not expect to receive anything from the Lord." –James 1:6-8

Branches: Doubting God's promises, Hesitating to pray or ask boldly, Fear of disappointment or unanswered prayers, Over reliance on logic or reasoning, Cynicism or skepticism, Trusting self over God, Inability to receive prophetic words or spiritual gifts, Rejection of supernatural ministry or healing, Shrinking from spiritual authority, Anxiety about the future, Disobedience rooted in fear or mistrust.

Reflections for the reader:

- What past experiences, disappointments, or wounds may have caused me to stop fully trusting God? (Be honest, has pain or waiting slowly silenced your faith?)
- In what areas of my life am I relying more on my own understanding than God's Word? (Reflect on what you protect, control, or overthink instead of surrendering.)

"But even before I was born,
God chose me and called me
by his marvelous grace.
Then it pleased him
to reveal his Son to me[a]
so that I would proclaim
the Good News about Jesus..."
-Galatians 1:15-16 (NLT)

10

The Impact of Loss

The author takes an unexpected turn with the death of the author's brother, which prompted him to return to New Jersey for the funeral. During this time, he delivered a powerful message about God's unwavering love, drawing parallels between his brother's life and the divine compassion extended to humanity. This experience solidified his purpose to help others find healing and redemption.

A Funeral Parallel and Paradox

*In memory of my sister Lisa Medina and my father Ceferino Medina.
In Dedication to my brother Jesus Medina*

One of the things that brought me to the end of myself was the day I took my son to karate class and had no clue how I got back home after drinking a pint of vodka. I woke up early the next morning, still in the car, my arms hanging over the steering wheel, but my son had made it home safe. It was like a light came on, and the thought hit me: If I had gotten into a car accident, I wouldn't have died, it's never the driver that dies, it's the passenger—and my son was the passenger. That hit me hard!

At that moment, no matter what I thought about God whether He was real or not—it didn't matter. I just looked up and said, "God, help me."

The very next day after that cry for help, someone came into my life and told me about Circle of Care, a program that helps people with problems like I had. They asked if I wanted to stay for seven days to detox. Of course, I felt ready—later, I would find out that I wasn't. Still, I agreed. When I sat down, it was like I was in another dimension. I looked up and saw a cloud, and in that cloud, I saw a picture of my dad and my sister. What I saw was them cheering me on.

I believe God allowed that to happen to help me take that first step forward because before my sister passed away, we had fought, and I never got to tell her how sorry I was for hurting her.

From seven days, I wound up staying thirty. After the seven days were over, the lady in the program asked if I wanted to stay another thirty days, and I knew I needed to. So I stayed.

After that, I left.

Now I have started working. I was in recovery. I was feeling the best I had ever felt, and about six months in, I said to myself, "I'm feeling good. I'm looking good. I've got a couple of dollars now. I think I'll go to Jersey and show them how good I'm doing."

At the time, I didn't know about pride, ego, or that it was an inside job. All I knew was that I was feeling good. Before I left, I swore on anything that I would never pick up again—and I truly believed it.

So I left for Jersey. Halfway there, a switch flipped in my thinking—and I had no control over the switch. It just came. The next thoughts were about what drug dealer I would see to get a bag. From that point on, everything went downhill.

After the relapse, I came back to Florida. Then came the guilt, the shame, the whys—and they almost kept me from going back to recovery. But I said, "God, I'm never going back to Camden, New Jersey, until You Yourself tell me that I'm ready." Because before that switch happened, I swore up and down that I wouldn't pick up again — but I did. And that kind of thinking is what I had to learn not to rely on anymore.

A year goes by. I ask God, "Can I go see my mother now?" and one way or another, He would tell me no. I took it as Him saying I wasn't ready.

Then year two.

Year three.

Year four.

Year five.

Year six.

Finally, on the seventh year, I get a phone call from New Jersey. My brother had passed away. After I hung up the phone, I cried out to God, asking, "Why did You take him? He was so young."

The only response I heard was, "Now you are going back. And you are not only going back—you are going to do the funeral service."

I said, "God, I'm not going up there to do no service. First of all, the last thing I want is for anyone to think I'm trying to take control of anything. Plus, the people in the hood don't want to hear about You anyway."

Now that I think about it, that sounded like an excuse. It reminded me of Moses when God told him to go to Pharaoh and say, "Let my people go," and Moses replied, "I'm not good at speaking." But God didn't ask him if he was. Just like He didn't ask me if they wanted to hear it or not.

So I said to God, "If this is even You speaking to me, You're really going to have to confirm it."

I got the plane ticket and headed to New Jersey. As I came down the stairway off the plane, the first thing I saw was four of my brothers at the bottom of the stairs. One of them—I hadn't seen or spoken to in years—the first words out of his mouth in a gangster voice: "Yo bro, we didn't get no one else to do it, no pastor, no preacher. You're gonna do it."

Right there and then, I knew God had spoken to me. That was the confirmation I asked God to give me and He did just that!

Days went by. I was getting nervous because I had never done anything like this before and didn't even know what I was going to say. Once again, I found myself crying out to God in desperation: "What do you want me to tell Your people?"

Suddenly, the atmosphere shifted. It was like God brought my brother's whole life before me—from the beginning to the end. Then I heard God say: "Your brother was with a woman who was very rebellious and stubborn. But no matter how stubborn she was, he never left her or his children. That's what I want you to tell My people: though they rebel against Me and are stubborn, I still love them. And just like he never left his family, I will never leave them."

The day of the service came and about 400 people showed up.

I started sharing what God had given me. It was so powerful that someone in the audience began speaking in tongues. As I finished, I heard God say, "Now give an altar call—yes, right here in the funeral home."

The atmosphere changed again. I knew every demon in that place had left. There wasn't one hand that didn't go up—meaning there wasn't one ear that didn't hear the Gospel and accept the Lord.

We didnt get anyone to sing but my cousin suddenly stood up and started singing in Spanish. The song lined up perfectly with the message: *"Who can separate us from the love of God?"*

And with that, the service ended—and I returned back home to Florida.

Understanding: I remember one day, talking with my brother, the one who has since passed away, and telling him, "One day, God is going to use us in a powerful way to help others." I knew deep in my heart that God was present in that conversation, and I believed it with everything in me. Later, I asked God about it. I said, "I thought You were going to use me and my brother to save others. I guess that wasn't You speaking at that time."

But then He answered me and said, "I did use both of you together to save lives. The difference was, you were standing, and he was in a casket. But you both were used together, and souls were drawn to the kingdom of heaven. So where he is, they will also be."

As the scripture says, "'My ways are not your ways, neither are your thoughts My thoughts,' says the Lord."

Spiritual Root: Unbelief

(Unbelief often partners with fear, rejection, and pride, and is at times passed generationally via religious or skeptical mindsets.)

Key Verses: *"Be careful then, dear brothers and sisters. Make sure that your own hearts are not evil and unbelieving, turning you away from the living God." –Hebrews 3:12*

"Lord, I believe; help my unbelief!" –Mark 9:24

"And without faith it is impossible to please God…" –Hebrews 11:6

"The one who doubts is like a wave of the sea… That person should not expect to receive anything from the Lord." –James 1:6-8

Branches: Doubting God's promises, Hesitating to pray or ask boldly, Fear of disappointment or unanswered prayers, Over reliance on logic or reasoning, Cynicism or skepticism, Trusting self over God, Inability to receive prophetic words or spiritual gifts, Rejection of supernatural ministry or healing, Shrinking from spiritual authority, Anxiety about the future, Disobedience rooted in fear or mistrust.

Reflections for the reader:

- What past experiences, disappointments, or wounds may have caused me to stop fully trusting God? (Be honest, has pain or waiting slowly silenced your faith?)
- In what areas of my life am I relying more on my own understanding than on God's Word? (Reflect on what you protect, control, or overthink instead of surrendering.)

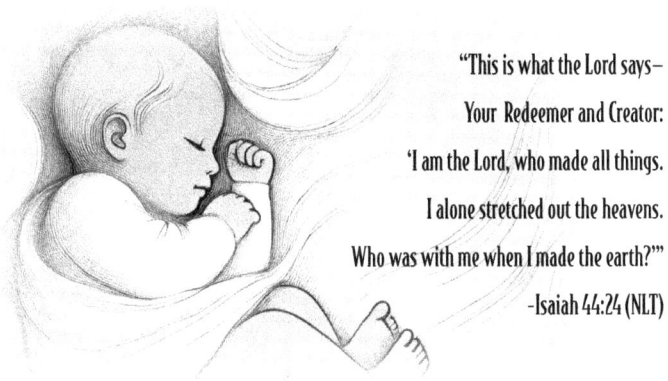

> "This is what the Lord says—
> Your Redeemer and Creator:
> 'I am the Lord, who made all things.
> I alone stretched out the heavens.
> Who was with me when I made the earth?'"
> —Isaiah 44:24 (NLT)

11

A Vision for the Future

The author concludes by sharing his vision of helping others from similar backgrounds by purchasing abandoned houses and providing job training. His journey illustrates the transformative power of faith and the importance of addressing the roots of pain to foster healing. He emphasizes that despite his past, God has a plan for his life, and he is committed to living out that purpose

Molded for the Vision

Later on, God gave me a vision. Part of it was to eventually go back and buy old abandoned houses, hire people from the city, and teach them how to work and take responsibility to help them find self-worth connected to hope and a future.

I didn't realize God had to first mold me into the vision before He could send me into it. In my head, it was going to happen right away. So I headed back to Jersey, still listening to my old way of thinking.

Now I'm there, looking around, and all of a sudden, fear takes over—a fear I now know was rooted in insecurity. I look around and say, "God, where is this money going to come from? The last thing I'm going to do is ask people for money; if that's the case, I'm not even going to do it."

After looking at properties, trying to find where the vision was supposed to happen, I realized I was still moving off a premature thought. The vision couldn't possibly be ready yet because I was still broken in areas of my life with no solid foundation for God to build on.

Like the Word says, "Unless the Lord builds the house, the builder builds in vain."

The next day, I got up and went to help someone clean their backyard outside of Camden. After I was done, I left and on my way back, all of a sudden, I felt a desire to wash my mom's car.

I'm sitting outside, waiting for the car to come through the wash, when a guy comes and sits next to me. We start talking, and I tell him that I used to live out here but moved to Florida, and that's where God began to change my life. I believed that one day He would send me back to help others who grew up like I did.

When the car was finished, I got up to walk toward it and as I'm walking away, I felt someone place something in my hand. I knew right away it was money. I didn't say, "Oh, you didn't have to do that." I instantly knew it was God.

The Understanding: Afterward, I heard God say, "This is how it's going to come. This is how it's going to happen — through people outside of Camden helping inside of Camden."

Spiritual Lesson

Key Verse: *"For the vision is yet for an appointed time, but at the end it shall speak, and not lie: though it tarry, wait for it; because it will surely come, it will not tarry." -Habakkuk 2:3 (KJV)*

Key Breakdown:

- **"Yet for an appointed time"** – God's promises have a precise, sovereign timing.
- **"At the end it shall speak"** – The vision will prove true and unmistakable.
- **"Though it tarry, wait for it"** – To human eyes, it may seem delayed, but faith calls for patience.
- **"It will surely come, it will not tarry"** – In God's time, it's perfectly on schedule—never late."

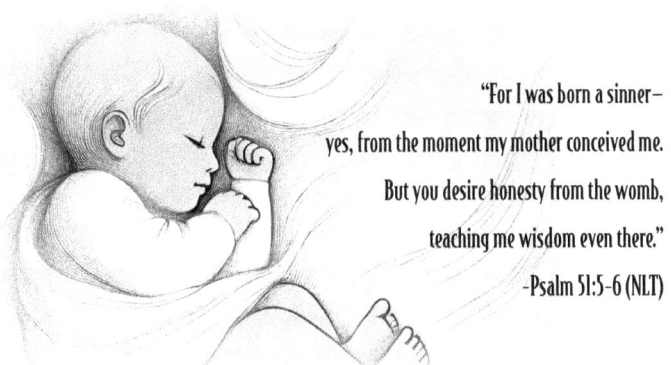

> "For I was born a sinner—
> yes, from the moment my mother conceived me.
> But you desire honesty from the womb,
> teaching me wisdom even there."
> -Psalm 51:5-6 (NLT)

12

A Heart Now Ready to Receive

The author's personal journey of faith over three years, culminated in a transformative experience during an Easter church service. The author describes feeling a divine call to give his heart to God, realizing that his previous beliefs were superficial due to a broken heart. This moment led to a newfound sense of freedom and a deeper understanding of his spiritual condition.

Encountering Jesus

After a while I'd say about three years of going to church and AA. I went to visit a church on Easter Sunday so I sat down at the worship and afterwards the preaching, then the altar call and while he was talking, I heard a voice say to me. "Now come to the altar and give me your heart" and I say to myself that couldn't be God, I already gave him my heart then I heard the voice say again, "Come to the altar and give me your heart."

I knew it was God, so I went to the altar and gave him my heart and after three years in recovery I experienced true freedom! I could breathe and life began to get so much better. That was the first time I realized how broken I really was, that even when I believed the lie that I had accepted the Lord in my life that it was a head thing because my heart was too broken to receive him, so all that time I was not under the influence of salvation but under the influence of a religious spirit that worked through a broken heart.

Spiritual Root: Religious Spirit
(Root or Fruit of a Wounded Identity)

Key Verse: *"These people come near to me with their mouth and honor me with their lips, but their hearts are far from me." –Isaiah 29:13*

Branches: Resistance to the Holy Spirit or new moves of God, Shame-based motivation for service, Fear of man disguised as righteousness, Legalism (obsession with rules, rituals, and outward conformity), Performance-based identity ("earning" God's love through works), Spiritual pride and superiority, Harsh judgment or criticism of others, Hypocrisy (appearing holy outwardly, disconnected inwardly) Obsession with appearance/reputation, Lack of compassion or mercy, Empty religious activity without intimacy with God.

Reflections for the reader:

- Have I ever tried to earn God's love or approval through religious activity, instead of receiving it by grace, understanding grace is a gift given and not earned? (Explore moments when doing for God replaced being with God.)

- In what ways have I judged others, elevated myself, or resisted the Holy Spirit's work out of fear or pride? (Let the Holy Spirit reveal subtle self-righteousness or fear-based control.)

Prayer

Heavenly Father, I didn't always have room for You.
My heart was too full of pain.
Too full of betrayal, shame, survival, and scars.
There were days I didn't want You.
And days I didn't believe You wanted me.

But You kept coming anyway.
Uninvited, but undeniable.
You stand in the wreckage.
You wait in the dark.
And now… I feel You knocking.

So today—I open the door.
Not with perfect faith,
But with a broken "yes."
Come in, God.
Come in and take the space I once filled with fear.
Fill what I emptied trying to protect myself.
Breathe, where it's still silent.
Burn, where it's still numb.

I don't just ask You to visit—I ask You to stay.

Cover me like only You can.
Not just with mercy… but with purpose.
Make this heart Your dwelling place.
And let what once held me down
become the ground You now rise from.

In Jesus' name, I now make room in my heart for you.
Amen.

Afterword

And so, my journey continues…

I've learned that God's ways are not our ways, and His thoughts are not our thoughts. He takes the broken and uses them for His glory, turning shame into strength, and pain into purpose. He reveals the roots of our pain so that we can be truly healed. He shows us that even in our darkest moments, He is there, sending "Moses" to deliver us, and angels of Grace and Mercy to protect us. He teaches us to walk by faith, not by sight, and to trust in His timing—not our own. He transforms our hearts, freeing us from the chains of unforgiveness and the lies of unworthiness. And He shows us that even in our weakness, He is strong, and that His love is powerful enough to overcome any obstacle.

About the Author

BERT CINTRON

Camden, NJ is where I'm from—son of Ceferino Medina and Gloria Cintron. My parents were born in Puerto Rico; I was born here in America. I went from their hands to the hands of the streets—streets that never showed me love. But back then, I didn't know any better. Now I do.

Before I was formed in my mother's womb, I was already on God's mind. He knew I'd have to walk through hell so that one day, He could pull me out of the darkness and into His marvelous light. Now, I speak to those still living in the dark I once called home. God rescued me—so I could help rescue you.

Book the Author for Speaking Engagements:

Call +1 (321) 215-1464

Follow the Author on Social Media:

YouTube @HeavenlyRealm-k8s

Facebook @HeavenlyRealm

**YOU WRITE,
WE PUBLISH,
TOGETHER WE CREATE**

DIVINE WORKS PUBLISHING, LLC.

We publish to inspire, inform, and transform—because your story was made to move hearts and shift minds.

At Divine Works Publishing, we publish purpose-driven writers and help bring their message to life.

www.DivineWorksPublishing.com

561-990-BOOK (2665)
info@ DivineWorksPublishing.com

www.ingramcontent.com/pod-product-compliance
Lightning Source LLC
Chambersburg PA
CBHW050044080526
44586CB00014B/1449